RIC MASTEN SPEAKING

Also by Ric Masten

Looking for Georgia O'Keeffe
Notice Me!
They Are All Gone Now...And So Are You
Even As We Speak
The Deserted Rooster
Stark Naked
Voice of the Hive
Dragonflies, Codfish, & Frogs
His & Hers (with Billie Barbara Masten)
Sunflowers

RIC MASTEN SPEAKING

RIC MASTEN

Papier-Mache Press, Watsonville, California

First Edition

Printed in the United States of America.

93   6 5 4 3 2

ISBN: 0-918949-11-4

The poems in this volume are largely reprinted from the following books: *Dragonflies, Codfish & Frogs, His & Hers, Voice of the Hive, The Deserted Rooster, Even As We Speak, They Are All Gone Now-and so are YOU,* and *Notice Me!*, published by Sunflower Ink and produced by Clack & Nichols; *Sunflowers*, published by Palo Colorado Press and produced by Clack & Nichols; *Stark Naked*, published by Sunflower Ink and produced by Nichols & Dimes; and *Looking for Georgia O'Keeffe and Other Observations*, published and produced by Sunflower Ink. "From the Shore," under the title "Who's Wavin'," and "Let It Be a Dance" also published as song lyrics by Mastensville Music Publishing, licensed through Broadcast Music, Inc. The individual copyright for all material in this volume rests with Ric Masten and poems may not be reprinted without permission from Ric Masten, Palo Colorado Canyon, Carmel, California 93923.

Cover art by Reed Farrington
Photographs by Marianne Gontarz
Cover design by Cynthia Heier
Edited by Sandra Martz

Library of Congress Cataloging in Publication Data.

Masten, Ric.
     Ric Masten speaking.
          p.   cm.
     ISBN 0-918949-11-4 : $8.00
     I. Title.
PS3563.A814R54 1990
811'.54—dc20

                                        90-33891
                                        CIP

To my mother, Hildreth,
my wife, Billie Barbara,
my daughters, Jerry, April, and Ellen
and my granddaughters, Cara and Gaia.

Foreword

As a child I would sit for hours with my most treasured possession, a bright colored cardboard cylinder that held tiny fragments of colored glass. Peering through the eyepiece, slowly turning the outer shell, I watched a succession of forms, an endless variety of colors. And it is thus that I think of these poems. Now you see an individualist, one who builds his home in the rugged Big Sur mountains; now a man-child of the '60s, recovering from alcohol addiction; now a little boy, riding a Flexible Flyer coaster, forever in the tall shadow of a father who died too young.

Speaking through the symmetry of poetry, Masten shows us life in its kaleidoscopic wonder. He is a lifelong student and a consummate teacher; a magician, a philosopher, a near-suicide; a man who has had successes and who has made mistakes and who survives.

As an editor most of my work has focussed on women, especially on those issues that affect midlife and older women. And yet this book does not seem at all out of place beside the others. I believe this is because he is a man who really *likes* women, who cares deeply about trying to find a way for women and men to communicate better. His work, influenced by the poetry of Anne Sexton, Sylvia Plath, and Stevie Smith, women who literally spent their lives trying to write their way out of the darkness, dares to show his vulnerability. Willing to say "I am afraid, I feel loneliness," here is a man who has dedicated his life to delivering the message: "You are not alone, alone."

I respect the poet. I am inspired by the man.

The material in this volume, drawn from twenty-five years of Masten's writing, is not presented chronologically but rather in a variegated pattern, allowing the reader to touch both the poet and his work. For those who have his other books, some of the poems will look a little different. And that is the mark of a speaking poet. Performed before live audiences, the poems are in constant revision, reflecting the changing phases and actions of both the speaker and the listener. Recognizing that many readers may never have the opportunity to hear Masten read his work aloud, Papier-Mache has also produced a *Ric Masten Speaking* cassette recording of a live concert performance featuring poems from this book.

And so, like the kaleidoscope, these are poems to return to, again and again, holding them up to life, peering through the eyepiece, an endless variety of forms, never seeing the same thing twice.

SANDRA MARTZ
EDITOR

Author's Note

i think of my poems and songs
as hands
if i don't hold them out to you
i find i won't be touched

if i keep them in my pocket
i will never get to see you
seeing me
seeing you

and though i know from experience
many of you
for a myriad of reasons
will laugh
and spit
and walk away unmoved
still
to meet those of you who do reach out
is well worth the risk
and pain

so
here are my hands
do what you will

Contents

1   Big Sur Country

3   An Encounter with Robinson Jeffers

4   Old Men

5   The Prisoners

6   With Birth to Look Forward To

8   A Tower

9   Strings Attached

10   The Wine

11   Murrey Stories

13   A Drinking Problem

15   Flags

16   Coming and Going

17   To Be a Housewife

18   A Suicide Attempt

20   No Strings

21   The Bixby Bridge Incident

24   Coming Home

26   Ellen

27   The Weaning

28   Grandparents and Grandchildren

30   A Loose End

32   The Exile

39   Beginning the Deathwatch

41   Last Words

43   Post-Rotational Nystagmus

45   Morning People vs Night People

49   Waterspots

51   A Small Quiet War

54   The Deserted Rooster

56   A Vanishing Species

58   Portrait of a Mother

59	Which Makes Me the Greatest Parent
60	Lifeline
65	Suddenly Grandsons
68	Days of Our Lives
71	The Quake of '89
73	A Magician
77	Airport Managers and Their Wives
78	Bad Taste
79	A Sleeper
81	The Deaf
84	A Bell Curve
86	Mississippi Jr. College Creative Writing Contest
88	The Way to Teach
90	Requiem
94	Looking for Georgia O'Keeffe
97	Pulitzer Prize Winner
98	Burnout
101	Happy Endings in the Badlands
104	Where the Poems Come From
106	A Farm Accident Years Ago
107	Whales
109	Wailing Wall
110	The Wasp Nest
112	From the Shore
113	Two Voices
114	For Anne Sexton
116	A California Mental Health Scene
120	Day of the Dogfish
128	The Orangutans
130	A Kind of Hope
131	Burning Truth
132	Even As We Speak
134	With a Friend Dying of Cancer
137	Let It Be a Dance

RIC MASTEN SPEAKING

Big Sur Country

it is called Big Sur country
where i live
and many men of letters have passed through
none have denied its beauty
but few have
felt at home here
old Henry Miller — city born
burned his bald head brown
trying to catch the color of the sun
at Partington
like Icarus
he failed and in the end
retired to a cement maze south of here
more at home in an elevator
than at those dizzy heights

and Jack Kerouac
hitched his way along this granite coast
with no real sense of belonging
crawling here like an ant
he found the place a graveyard
the offshore rocks
tombstones
in a ghostly surf
on the road
running like a child in the dark
hearing things in the bushes
he hurried north to hide
in the mulch pits of Marin County

1

and Richard Brautigan has come and gone
and others
drawn to and driven off
by the size and silence of this place
but Jeffers knew
that soaring old predator
sharp-eyed
he knew
if we could speed time up
fast enough
we would see that the mountains
are dancing
and with us

An Encounter with Robinson Jeffers

i found him reflecting
in his stone tower
alone
his profile against the window
poet
why so silent in these your latter days
have you nothing more to say?

i was coming on strong — fat
with young ideas
beating the bushes
shooting at everything in sight
he turned his face to mine

when you have said
what it is you have to say
and played all the obvious variations
you will learn to sit quietly
in the afternoon
and listen to the thicket

thus i left him
just off the trail
an old hunter
waiting for the game
to come to him
one shell
left
in the chamber

Old Men

the one from Colorado
stares from faded denim eyes
and lets the sound of a taxi
lift
and carry him back
to mountains
larger than life

the one from Indiana
keeps corn seed in his pocket
after the rain
his fingers
crawl on the pavement
earthworms
searching for cracks

i
am a Californian
and when my time comes
i will take off my coat
sit in the sun
and dream of the foothills
the sleeping lions

The Prisoners

though i have seen the photographs
of those ragged weary men
still i think i envy them
the prisoners
captured in a good
and holy war
which every war has been

caught and confined
by an obviously evil enemy
left to rot in some forgotten
prison camp
stubbornly clinging to secret information
for which i'd rather die than tell
surviving in a roach- and rat infested cell
my eye fixed
on that thin sliver of hope
at the edge of the door
the crack of light
that keeps us alive
in our solitary confinement

yes — there have been times
i've wished it were a simpler prison
for out here
in this open field of sunshine
it is far
far more difficult
to plan the great escape

With Birth to Look Forward To

would it be easier
to live life in reverse
like a video tape rewinding

oh i'm sure
it would take some getting used to
walking backward that way
things constantly flying into my hands
but if i could start at the end
putting death behind me
at the beginning
just think of that!

going to sleep each night
waking up a little younger
mind clearing
strength returning
able to thread a needle
and throw a fastball again

and desire
stirring like a summer breeze at first
the flag barely moving
then flying triumphant
in the prevailing winds

as the days lengthen however
i realize

i am trading away lived experience
for adolescent energy
and a full head of hair

suddenly
my father comes back to life
and once again
i take him for granted
i begin to shrink
until sinking to my knees
i roll over in my crib
and wave good-bye to my feet

stripped of all identity
toothless and bald again
i slip back inside my mother
to dissolve in the absolute darkness
of never having been

A Tower

i had a vision once
of a tower
here on the shoulder of this mountain
and i went wild
with a hammer and a dream

but don't be overly impressed
with those of us who build towers
any number of journeymen carpenters
and stonemasons
can tell you how to do it

the building part is easy
it's the living in it
that comes hard

with some simple instruction
anyone can hang a door
but if you know the art
of oiling hinges

teach me

Strings Attached

i have given gifts
trinkets
inexpensive tokens of my affection
but with instructions
that you must pass them along
give them away
to someone you love and admire

and when you do
i am crushed

The Wine

the vintners speak lovingly
of the compatible enzyme
in a fine table burgundy
and how it works
with candlelight and crystal
to keep an evening gracious

and
then there are those
two-dollar-a-gallon
straight-from-the-bottle
dago red times
when i'm never sure
who's talking
you or the wine

and
it's not that i minded
sorting through all the junk you dumped
i probably deserved it
but in that last minute
if i hadn't caught your coat
do you think
you really would have jumped?

Murrey Stories

on the eve
of his military induction
half-swacked
a bunch of us took Murrey
out to where Fast Frances lived
cracking up
as he thrashed in the ivy
climbing to her second-story window

"go away Murrey you're drunk!"

and laughing madly
shouting Batmaaaannnnnnnn!
he launched himself out
into the night
a short flight that ended badly
on the business end of a garden spigot

gored by a rampaging Rainbird!
he whooped
as an unamused
Emergency Ward doctor attempted to close
the foolish grin in his scrotum

at dawn
we passed the jug around
said our good-byes
then watched him board the Greyhound
gingerly keeping his legs

in the exact shape of a croquet hoop
next afternoon he was back
waiting for us
at the Cork & Bottle
out on a short medical deferment
a length of time that became
the celebration
none of us remember anything about

oh
the tales we love to tell!

a close friend
even going to the trouble
of building a small redwood deck
off his living room
a place he claims
created specifically for the two of us
to have a martini
and tell our Murrey stories on

yesterday
somewhat wistfully he mentioned
that the space has not been used
since i began recovering

12

A Drinking Problem

RSVP—and we do respond don't wc?
gussying up for the grand event
the stepsisters
dressing and undressing
the prince breathing into his hand
testing his breath
Rapunzel with her fine-tooth comb
insecurity
working like a worm in a winesap

all that time and attention
all that fuss and bother
that mirror mirror on the wall business
all that
just to gct past self-duubt
and on to the gala affair
where above the noise and din
someone can shout

come on in
and name your poison

and we do respond don't we?

the worm turning here
to quickly demolish the reflected image
that had seemed so important in the glass
on the outside of the door
the spit and polish dissolving
in the glass on the inside till

Cinderella is out of her shoes
the heir to the throne
puking on the floor
and coming undone before our eyes
Rapunzel
really letting her hair down

and don't think you can avoid
the transformation
by avoiding the drink
in situations such as these
a nondrinker has a drinking problem too

my abstinence
making me appear to you like a grumpy giant
a bad-tempered troll
my sobriety
taken as a clear reflection on present company
and when Snow White is into the apples
she wants nothing to do with a mirror

Flags

she dresses in flags
and comes on
like a Mack truck
she paints
her eyelids green
and her mouth
is a loudspeaker
rasping out profanity

at cocktail parties
she is everywhere
like a sheep dog
working a flock
barking
nipping at your sleeve
spilling your drink
bestowing
wet sloppy kisses

but i
have received
secret messages
carefully written
from the shy
quiet woman
who hides
in this bizarre
gaudy castle

Coming and Going

i have noticed
that men
somewhere around forty
tend to come in from the field
with a sigh
and removing their coat in the hall
call into the kitchen

you were right
Grace
it ain't out there
just like you've always said

and she
with the children gone at last
breathless
putting her hat on her head
the hell it ain't!

coming and going
they pass
in the doorway

To Be a Housewife

i have in my life
stepped out on my wife
and tried waiting
in a white room
for a young working woman
to bring me color
through a white door

it has been a long morning
with this blank piece of paper
and quiet guitar

a stripe of sunlight
begins to explore the carpet
i watch it with no more on my mind
than you
and this slow unwinding lonely time

you will come soon for lunch
i will hear your sound in the hall
your hand on the latch
and then time will fly
till you're off to work again
and i am left alone again
washing the afternoon walls with my eyes
my god
to be a housewife waiting
always waiting
and you can't create while waiting
you can only wait

A Suicide Attempt

a story always loses something
in the second telling
and so
over the years the Graftons
developed a relationship
that needed a third party around
to break the silence

if the children behaved
and the job was secure
if no one had died
and the car didn't knock
they lived with the sound of the traffic outside
and the clock

Myrna survived
with the Jr. League and a Brownie troop
and when the kids grew up she went into group
Charlie held on playing golf
till his back wouldn't let him
then feeling his age one day
left home and flew to Cleveland on business
checking into a motel
as a Mr. and Mrs. Smith
but like the sales pitch says
after one night in a Holiday Inn
you'll not be surprised in the next

in retrospect i think the whole affair
was a kind of suicide attempt
on something gone humdrum
and Charlie going to sleep that night
vaguely wondered
if the maid would arrive in time to turn off the gas
if she did
perhaps it would be a good omen
if not —
well a story always loses something
in the second telling

No Strings

kites are one thing
but i have noticed the birds
have no strings
and whether it is true or not
doesn't matter
but i have looked upon you
as a wounded sparrow
to be lifted and cupped in my hand
careful not to touch your broken wing

and there were times when you pecked me
viciously
over things i could not fathom
but then god knows what a sorry sight
i made
bending over you in such concerned pity
so i left the cage open
hoping you'd be off

and suddenly it comes to my attention
how the front door
has been carefully left ajar

i notice this
as the morning sun
is pouring across the floor
and if either of us should fly
without a song
it will all have been for nothing

20

The Bixby Bridge Incident

the cup looked half empty
the big hand said forty-two past
and the word if there was one
was tired
then suddenly the wind touched my hair
and i became aware of myself
there on the bridge
a weary old bird ready to leap
from the nest and fly blind
to the breathing sea below

me
in my best bulky-knit sweater
calmly inching forward
a great sadness
in my blue-grey eyes
hair blowing
aware now
i paused and listened to the night
for motor sound
and looked for lights
but the world was empty
no one was coming to witness
my final scene
the grand finale
and it was such a fantastic
dramatic moment

i decided to come back
and tell you all about it
laughing
shaking my head
i drove home
but it wasn't until i saw the shape
of my own house
that i discovered the cup
had been half full
all the time

i was told recently
that of all witnessed suicides
from the Golden Gate Bridge
in San Francisco, California
not one
not a single person
has been seen to go off on the ocean side
the horizon side
all
as of this writing
have been seen leaping back
toward the city
and that would be a hell of a thing
to discover half way down

once years ago
i hung by my heels
was swatted — whaaaaah — and decided
to suck air and live

on a bridge near Big Sur, California
in the summer of '71
i faced the same decision again
and as i write this
i realize
i am
three months old today

Coming Home

the continuing story of a traveling salesman
continues
this time
we find him running
out of an airport gift shop
with a cap pistol
and a doll
a surprise for the kids
but like oxfords
hastily bought
a size too small
(the kids i remembered
were not kids at all)

i think i've been gone longer than i thought
cried
old Saint Nick
as ever ho-ho-hoing
as ever coming and going
giving the children puppies for Christmas
never there when the dog died

but it's okay dad
it's all right
they say
there is no such thing
as a bad parent

24

they say
even people who batter their offspring
are doing the best
they know how to do

and you can tell that
to the boxes that were never opened

you can tell that to the shoes that pinch

Ellen

my youngest daughter
likes to ride
to the mailbox with me
she fetches the mail
while i turn the car around
then she climbs into the back seat
and doles out my letters
slowly
inspecting each envelope
till i am infuriated
and turn red
and shout at her
Ellen!
gimme
the letters!

my youngest daughter likes to do this
it is one of the few times
she has my full attention

26

The Weaning

after considerable work in the field
i have come to the conclusion
that when it comes to me
and my children
it is easy to say "no" all the time
and it is easy to say "yes" all the time
but it is impossible
to be a logical consistent parent

however
i do not lie awake nights
over this any longer
for to treat children
in a logical consistent fashion
and then turn them out into the world
as we know it
would be a cruel crippling
and inhuman thing to do

it is only fair though
that when the kids have broken loose
and are out on their own
they should receive a handwritten letter
from me their father
expressing my love
and stating that all is forgiven
if they promise not to come home

Grandparents and Grandchildren

trying hard to understand human nature
i
having pacifist leanings
find my son learning karate
breaking bricks with his bare hands
so that he could kill a man in two seconds
he says smiling
as i go up the wall

and i
being the son of militant ex-Catholic
atheist parents
get myself ordained a minister
much to the disgrace of my old mother
whose reedy voice calls me on the phone

Ricky! — she squeaks
as always speaking
like a Punch and Judy show
and i as always looking
for the alligator to jump up
and hit her with a stick

Ricky! — she squawks
you're not gonna let them
put Reverend in front of your name
in the phone book are you?

now
i suppose
all this explains
why the grandparents and the grandchildren
usually get along so well

they have a common enemy

A Loose End

it's true i've put off
dealing
with one aspect of my father's life
a loose end so to speak
perhaps because he died when i was so young
and i remember him not so much as a person
but more of a presence
a feeling

so it's not him that i must
finally
get around to—rather the end of him
he was forty-nine when he passed away
i was twelve—he seemed older than God then
but now with me at forty-six i can see
he was in his prime and his
untimely
death is what really has me
bothered
the shadow of this event just ahead
the date crossing my path—an open fracture
in the shape of a question mark
i ask myself
could i ever be older than
my father?

and a kind of panic
fills me
to break through the barrier
and find myself alone on the other side
without him
i think i'd rather die first
and in the next three years if i'm not careful
this could be the loaded gun that just might
kill me

The Exile

THE SITUATION

tidying up
after the requiem
mother shipped my father East
his ashes swept beneath
a corner of her family's
family stone

New England
is glorious in the Fall
she wept
and he'll be with the Phinneys
and the Pratts

but half a century
two more husbands
and a ship's captain later
(it's difficult to imagine
the breathless multitude awaiting
her favors on the other side)
she changed her mind

and when the dust settled
it was not
in that illustrious cemetery
on the East Coast
but at the foot
of a California redwood
close enough to her offspring

to keep us all
talking to a ghost
in death
as well as life
she kept to her favorite aphorism
"out of sight — out of mind"

and like a pea
under forty-three mattresses
my father's situation
began to bother me

INCIDENT AT MOUNT AUBURN

but why?
when so many would gladly die
for the privilege of being buried
with all this Boston money
why
would you want your father exhumed?

the puzzled funeral director
threw up his hands
as i held the man at finger point
backing from the room
like a bandit
making off with a strongbox

outside
slapping my thighs
to sound like galloping horses
i ran for the wagon
a hail of imaginary bullets
kicking up dirt
in the asphalt parking lot
a nonexistent posse in hot pursuit
we shot through the ornamental gates
hightailing it out of there
a split second before closing time

34

in reality
the incident described
was businesslike
and most undramatic
a simple matter
of goods and services
bought and sold

but in traffic
that goes anywhere near my father
i drive
a Flexible Flyer coaster
and am never more
than twelve years old

VIEWING THE ASHES

who knows what i expected
something that would blow
away in the wind
i suppose
not a box of sand
and shell fragments

although
if i were insect size
i'd walk this chalky dune
hands clasped behind — eyes downcast
sifting the bits and pieces
searching for a chambered nautilus
that wasn't broken
common sense telling me
i might as well be looking
on the moon

still
if such a thing should exist
i'll find it
and put it to my ear
picking up the conversation
where you left it

CONCLUSION AT WILDCAT COVE

once
the handsome house
that crowns the shelf of rock
at Wildcat Cove
was home

my father
set the Spanish tile himself
and built the garden wall
with stones
hauled up from the beach below

since then
the property has changed hands
so many times
i can only guess who stands
at the window now
looking down wondering
what these trespassers
have buried in the sand
my brother and i
buccaneers again
return to a childhood playground
and at the base of a once-familiar cliff
place
like pirate treasure

the small brass chest
where only we could find it

and even though
the eulogy began and ended
with the words "what if?"
something more
than a shovelful of dust
was finally put to rest

later
leaving the experience
i reach a place far enough away
to have some real perspective
and looking back
see where our footprints
cross
a section of the beach
and realize
for the very first time
that the line continues on
out of sight
in both directions

Beginning the Deathwatch

Mother
has spent most of her adult life
in California
but like elephants
well-to-do ladies
from Brookline, Massachusetts
know exactly
where their bones should lie

when I die
pack me off to Mount Auburn
don't just sack and scuttle me
out here on the West Coast

and there is something else
i've recently learned
about elephants
they prefer to face death alone

no need to come home
you know how your younger brother
exaggerates

this counterpoint to:
she refuses to see us
i think the radiation
is killing her

and what can you say to that
long distance
except how bad you feel
not being there to help
hoping they won't suspect
how glad you are that you aren't
and following this
the guilt

but life is never easy
and what was once the size of a fist
shrunk to the size of a pea
and this medical miracle
puts me right back in line
behind
a trumpeting old pachyderm
who loves the circus
too much
to ever give up her ivory

Last Words

"tell us Gertrude, what's the answer?"
and it is reported
that the wily old poet
spent her last breath whispering
"what's the question?"

and being
the same kind of irrepressible exotic
i had expected as much from you Mother
at least
i was looking for something
more quotable than
"hurry along now
or you'll miss your movie"
but when mamma's gone
a mamma's boy is free
to rearrange reality
and end your story with a more
dramatic scene played earlier that day

the one in which you groaned
tugging feebly
at the cloth restraint that held you
in what you must have known
would be your deathbed
saying "cut me loose Ricky
cut me loose"

Mother
in this as in all things involving you
i can now
remember what i want to remember
and forget what i need to forget

Post-Rotational Nystagmus

the phenomenon occurs
when you look away from a moving object
and get the feeling you're traveling
in the opposite direction

with this in mind
know that my late mother
took great pleasure in predicting
that one day
i'd see the conservative light
in the end
i'll have your bleeding heart
she'd say
like the sorceress queen in Snow White

her basket
overflowing with polished apples
such as Richard Nixon was an American saint
and oh how she'd cackle
from behind her right wing
when i'd bite

and aside from throwing tantrums
the only recourse i had
was to keep the beard growing
and guarantee
that on election day

she could count on me
to cancel out her vote
it was that kind of child/parent
relationship
that is
until she went off
to the great Republican Party in the sky
leaving me
with a small diversified portfolio
hardly a ticket to Easy Street
but enough
for the "down side"
to make me feel queasy
while watching the broad tape run

enough
to recognize the sound of a last laugh
when i hear one

Morning People vs Night People

according to morning people
night people are necrophiliacs
lying dead to the world
coming to life only when the light fails
hinged at the waist
lifting slowly like coffin lids
they rise pale as the moon
to go about their dark murky business
their mad jerky dance
till the crack of dawn
has them cowering back behind a hand
shrinking from the very thought
of a hearty breakfast
creeping away
they sleep with salamanders
while morning people shower
brush their teeth and rush to meet the day

to night people however
morning people seem to be
perverted jogging machines
getting off on self-punishment
kinky types — sweaty — breathing hard
in love with their own shoes
flagellators
whipping themselves along
with an unsmiling determination
that smacks of Hitler's Youth

listen!
there is something rather Nazi
about a flat belly
and something terribly immoral about people
who go to bed with John Chancellor

either way
it's really not a question of wrong or right
it's just that some demons
won't let you sleep in the morning
and some demons keep you awake in the night

Waterspots

yes
even Sergeant York missed occasionally
and i'm told by certain female intimates
that all across the civilized world
women have mopped — muttering
if the target is that hard to hit
why can't a man making his stand
just sit?

however women
a musketeer's aim and marksmanship
are not the problem here
as in the game of darts
dead center is not
where the big points are scored
it's the half inch of *silence*
at the edge of the pond
the thin strip of porcelain
and flirting this way with the rim
even an expert can't be expected
to keep all of his darts on the board

i don't know who made up the rules
or why
but for some reason prudence
prefers the hush of the hard surface
to the voice of the laughing pool
which makes no sense at all men
considering the symphony we go through

whistling and coughing
and clearing our throats
when intruders approach in the hall
why not simply
let 'em know we're in there
with the sweet sound of a waterfall?

now there's a liberating thought!

from this day forward
i shall let the work speak for itself
and by so doing
show some real concern for the cleanup crew
killing two birds with one stone
my sights as well as my consciousness raised

i for one
will blaze away at the bull's-eye
a welcome visitor
known by women the world over
as a straight shooter

50

A Small Quiet War

over the years my wife and i
have discovered two things
a man and a woman
should avoid doing together
that is
if they value their relationship
laying rugs
and carrying mattresses

and she's at it again
my wife
under the house digging

i can hear her down there
with my old rusty tools
picking and shoveling away
hollowing out a place
for her imagination to run wild in

she's been at it off and on now
for two years
running back and forth
with one shovel full of dirt at a time
throwing it into the yard
doing it the hard way
and i must admit
i'm always a bit surprised
and annoyed

when i see the size of the pile
she is making
but it's her project and she says
i'm not
and don't have to be involved

still and all
it has now become impossible
for me to lie here comfortably
listening to the ball game

The Deserted Rooster

if this were a documentary
Lorne Greene would narrate
describing in his big male animal world way
the migration
as one by one the fledglings flew the coop
followed by the hen
liberated and running off to join the sisters
cloistered in the halls
of a community college
singing
Gloria
Gloria
Steinem — till it becomes catholic

so far nothing new
children leaving home
a woman's victory
over the empty nest syndrome
themes done to death

but the deserted rooster is a subject
that has not yet been addressed
we know him
only as that laughable old strutter
preening and parading up and down
involved in his sexual prowess
and the sound of his own voice
up
at an ungodly hour to start the day

54

it was all part of the job
and there wasn't a problem
when there wasn't a choice

but picture him now
after the exodus
all alone
scratching around in his abandoned domain
looking for a good reason to get up tomorrow
and crow

if this were a documentary
it would end
focused on a stereotype weather vane
rusted on the turning point

in a changing wind

A Vanishing Species

i was born on a planet
over fifty light-years from here

an idyllic world
where children grew up
without the threat of nuclear holocaust
or ecological strangulation
no instant systems of communication
no black revolutions
gay revolutions
drug revolutions
no women's liberation
not even the choice
of taking or not taking the pill
an Eden really

true
the seed of all this was there
but had nothing to do
with my first fifteen years

and now
i find myself come to this harsh place
a kind of space traveler
having close encounters with my own children

like creatures
from different star systems
we stare at each other
across the void
even our words have different
stems

we are aliens in each other's midst

but damn it
i am the one saddled with the memory
of that other place
part of a colony
stranded on the planet earth
toward the end of the twentieth century
marooned
with no way to go back
and no time to go on

like a moon being eclipsed
my kind will soon be gone
and in light
of the headlines today
the sooner the better

Portrait of a Mother

what's a mother to do
when a son
with no visible means of support
wears Salvatore Ferragamos
drives a Maserati
and makes payments
on a two-thousand-dollar-a-month apartment

what else
but wonder out loud
about the enormous diamond ring
even Liberace
would have found tasteless
"don't worry Mom
it costs a lot less
than you'd think"

and for the life of me
she mused
laughing darkly
i can't decide
whether that was the good
or the bad news

Which Makes Me the Greatest Parent
Who Ever Played the Game

in the major league
of Child Psychology
the heavy hitters claim
you can tell how well
you managed as a parent
by the ease
with which your children
steal away from home

this being the case
don't you wish
parenting
were more like the real
game of baseball
wherein at least
if you bat a career .500
you go to the Hall of Fame

Lifeline

he sits
the picture of impatience
foot jerking
ready to split the moment he arrives
busy busy
always in a desperate kind of hurry
with nothing to show for his time
utopia just a day away
radiant one moment — desolate the next
my only son
a textbook example
of someone in trouble at the deep end

however
the school of lived experience
has taught me
that to dive into a pool of denial
trying to go to the rescue
only results
in two codependent fools
floundering around
overboard in the Bermuda Triangle

no
this time all i'm willing to do
is throw in a lifeline
making absolutely certain
he knows where it is
beyond this it's up to him

Son
the local number
for Narcotics Anonymous is 624-2055
sink or swim

Suddenly Grandsons

the orphans of dysfunction
appear on our doorstep
three small bewildered refugees
five
seven and ten
coming to us
through the auspices of a marriage
dismantled by codependence
and substance abuse
Mommy
dwindling down to a few evasive
calls from the East
Dad
unraveling locally
looking in taprooms for self-esteem
counseling with barkeeps
hard-pressed to find time
for the traditional
good night boys
sweet dreams
and don't let the bedbugs bite

sadly
at this juncture
there is no light at the end of the tunnel
just the stunning enormity of recent events
the night tear-streaked at first

Grandma
punishing her pillow with a fist
damn it
i've already done this!
i'm not a child-rearing machine
life must be more
than picking toys up off the floor
more than making boys make beds
being resented and unappreciated
(then the saving grace of laughter)
that is until after
one of them becomes a famous author
and like Truman Capote
pens a moving
childhood remembrance of me...
of course by then i'll be dead

for Gramps an opposite reaction
here was an opportunity
to beat myself black and blue
building forts—hanging swings
doing things
i didn't do the first time around

oh—
as an organ donor
the kids had my kidney lungs and heart
but not the kind of attention it takes
to make a coaster and fix a bike

nowadays however
the career runs on competence
not blind ambition
which leaves plenty of time
for catch and kites
and also unhappily
time for thoughts that disturb and demean
like how much of this situation
results directly
from my having been
an absentee parent off chasing a dream
in any case
Gramps and Grandma
are doing as well as can be expected
valiantly trying not to forget
that these dear little troopers
really don't belong to us
and that like it or not
the future depends entirely
upon the action and reaction
of two loose cannons

as the butt
of what is fast becoming
an all-too-familiar joke
we are just two more senior citizens
taking it one day at a time
in the Loony Tune atmosphere
of boing-boing ka-boom!
eh—what's up doc?
and th-th-that's all folks!

Days of Our Lives

the trial separation fails—
the Duke and Duchess of denial
reconcile
rather than deal with loneliness
it seems
the codependent hard core
prefer to live in hell
and i can live with that

what's difficult to live with
is the thought of my grandsons
back eating Rice Crispies
off the floor of a dark grungy flat—
cranking up the TV to drown out
the sound of parents at war

a bumper-car kid i know
now grown
assures me that every foster child
treasures that brief stay in a positive situation
without it she says
she would never have known the difference
between quarrel and conversation—
clutter and filth

this however
doesn't erase the painful memory
of three
understandably happy boys
running with sleeping bags

piling into
that patched-up situational wreck
Gramps and Grandma
standing in the rain
waving good-bye off the deck

if it all begins
to resemble a cornball soap opera
i'm sorry
but real life is like that
a happy ending depending entirely
upon where you check in
and out
of the ongoing story

The Quake of '89

the ride up
the bumpy country road to our place
must measure at least 7.1 on the Richter
because i missed it completely
pounding the dashboard
attempting to reclaim a lost baseball game
i rounded a corner to find family and friends
jumping up and down
arms waving wildly
and until i saw the whites of their eyes
i just naturally assumed
they were that glad to see me

inside
it had rained knickknacks
my spouse keeping on display
every trinket and gimcrack
that has ever come her way
and sad to say
nothing was broken
except one hideous
(the adjective she would dispute)
bird-shaped bottle of cheap perfume
which has magically transformed our home
into a house of ill repute

71

of course
from the Bay Area and Santa Cruz
come the real horror stories
and yet
even for us who would lose
little more than the use of the phone
and a few hours of electricity
even for us
the quake has taken its toll
my sense of security
shaken from its tenuous underpinning
the grand illusion
that i am in control
wrecked
gone the way of the I-880 Cypress Project

since 5:04 p.m.
October 17th
it no longer seems odd at all
that the notion of an evil conspiracy
is easier to live with
than the thought
of an off-the-wall act of God

A Magician

hey
how do you do that?
this
after my Uncle Jimmy
made a penny disappear
then smiling slyly found it again
in my ear

now to a seven year old
this is the stuff of which
the meaning of life is made
and i begged him to reveal the mystery
and teach me to do it
and when he did i could see
there wasn't much to it
except practice
and the fact that through it
i became the undisputed star
of the second grade
which was all right
but making the magic
is never as much fun
as watching it being made

we all love a magic show
and want to become a magician
and in a way we do
each of us developing a life style
creating an illusion
with a line of patter

a trick or two
working within
a setting of our own design
getting good enough to spellbind
at least a few
into catching their breath
as they enter our life saying
hey how do you do this?

and it works for a while
and it's fun for a while
till the day you discover yourself
doing some sleight of hand
even you don't quite understand
and in order to be on top
of your own act
you take it apart carefully

only to learn
that like the penny the loneliness
and anxiety
never really did vanish
it was just that during the performance
you forgot about it
but then knowing how to do the stunt
is not what keeps a real magician going

what keeps him going
has always been
the "oooohs" and "ahhhhs"
and anyway would you really
want to walk around
with a penny in your ear?

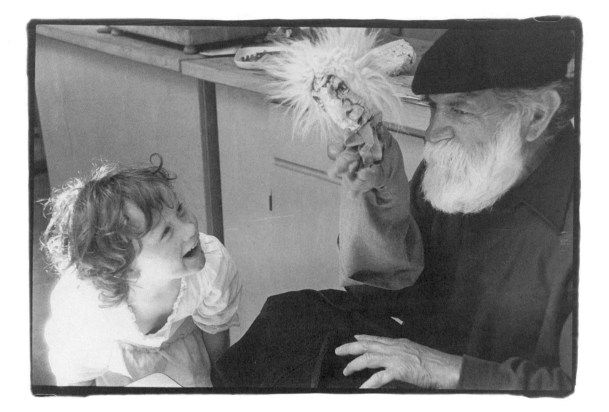

The Poet Addresses the Western United States Regional Conference of Airport Managers and Their Wives

when i arrived the microphone and stool
said Barry Manilow
when they should have been saying
Robert Bly

the chairman of the program committee
suggesting
that if i would also play guitar during dinner
there'd be an extra fifty in it for me

to which i responded
with a quick thumbnail sketch
of Vachel Lindsay

later
after the welcome
the awards
and the election of new officers
i was tendered to an audience
filled with Tony Bennett expectations

and for thirty intoxicating minutes
i was the only person
on the face of the earth
who knew
what was coming next

Bad Taste

hanging above
her purple Naughahyde couch
was the bullfighter
painted on black velvet

don't you just love
the way it seems to glow?
she said

and then went on to say
that she considered me
to be
one of the finest poets
writing in America today

A Sleeper

to be a poet reading
is chancy work at best
tough enough to face rejection
but worse
far worse this

you fell asleep
even as i read you closed your eyes
and dropped your head upon your chest
and to this day i marvel
that you kept your seat
nodding east and west

and although i find it sad
i guess it's only human
that looking back upon a sea
of open faces
i can best recall the one that slept
and wonder
were you overtired
or simply bored
with all that i expressed

only now writing this
years later
have i thought to ask about the dream
you might have had that day
and all
i may have missed

The Deaf

imagine a woodsman
swinging an axe in the distance
the tree speaking out of sync
then nothing
except what is left in your eye
chips still fly
but your ears
dumb fleshy things
hang from your head
useless handles frozen stiff

the world around you
fills with dead air
the quiet thickens
till the atmosphere is packed solid
surrounding you like clear wax
and everyone there
rides in a limousine
stars of the silent screen
seen through shatterproof glass
the faces glide past
lips moving like goldfish

the trumpet has lost its voice
the seashell — mute as a dish

my god
in a place like this
what do you do with a word
like inconceivable?

spell it she said
hands moving behind the question
in a kind of semaphore
and you talk too fast

later that evening
the poems fell from my mouth
little naked birds
crying for life
and who would have known
they were there
had she not taken them into her care
holding them up
till they could fly on their own

and back where this began
the tree came crashing down
and the sound
was the sound
of the deaf
applauding

A Bell Curve

if your carpenter
didn't know what batterboards were
you are probably living in a lopsided house
the carpenter's apprentice
will carry and stack a lot of lumber
learning his trade

and when it comes to brain surgeons
i believe in grades
bell curves and all that
i want to see him flunked out
long before he gets into my head
asking a nurse
what all the funny looking wrinkled stuff is
and God help the electrical engineer
who gets his wires crossed

but how do you grade a poem?

i mean wouldn't it be a little bit
like trying to grade a dream

ah — student
your dream started off well enough
but fell all apart in the middle
too much sex for sex's sake
and the ending was quite frankly trite
at best this is a C- dream

84

parents — faculty — students — friends
what we have here is the finest trade school
in the history of the world
period
so let's hear it for today's tool and die makers
and leave the dreamers be

Mississippi Jr. College Creative Writing Contest

for the entrants

it being the South
the expectation was
that some unborn Capote
would leap from the competition
and take me by the throat
or
that i would find myself
forgiving
an adolescent Katherine Anne Porter
for being a bit sophomoric
my picky criticism
punctured
by at least one poignant phrase

the reluctant judge
amazed in the end
and delivered by a painfully green
yet promising James Dickey

alas
this was not to be
for either
i have gone blind
(always a possibility)
or
the needle in the haystack
simply wasn't there to find

86

in any case
i can only wonder now
would it have been easier
to pick an ace
from a pack of aces?
tomorrow
some latent William Faulkner
may emerge from all of this
and prove me wrong
but not sorry
a critic is never sorry
for
if you let my red pen
turn you from your love of language
to a desolate and dreary life
pumping gas
then that
is where you belong

The Way to Teach

it isn't so much having a question to ask
rather the ability to create one

and so
he let them have their games
until the tide was fully out
and when it was
he came upon the rocky beach
a maypole of a man
among the shouting children
and bending down beside a magic pool
peering in
he waited

he waited till a ring of faces gathered
at the edge of this attention
then slowly reaching through the mirror
gave a sea anemone
a punch
who did what sea anemones will do
quickly folding in
on what should have been a lunch
WOW!
he said — eyes popping
then abruptly rising
but keeping in mind the length of his legs
moved on up the beach
the children scrambling behind
with questions

Requiem

for Sharon Christa McAuliffe

some say that you
and the Challenger crew
came to a tragic end
but when i recount the story
of your star-crossed flight
when i describe the circumstance
surrounding your death
i will do so in the same breath
i use to tell about a comic
who died
at the height of his career
on stage cracking a joke
the laugh still building

and so dear teacher
the tears are not for you
but for an assembly
of cheering high school students
there to wish you bon voyage
it was Times Square New Year's Eve
until the explosive arrival
of childhood's end
the premature loss of innocence
caught
wearing a birthday party hat
clutching a tin kazoo

no dear teacher
the tears are not for you

90

the grief i feel
is for the other finalists
the nine who just missed the boat
one minute wrestling with envy
the next flooded with relief
countervailing emotions
separated only
by a startling puff of smoke
the castaways drenched with guilt
at what they felt
when the call came
and they were granted
that last minute reprieve
i grieve for them dear teacher
not for you

but most of all i'm angry
at myself for being fascinated
by the telescopic view
of your forlorn family
huddled on the dock
waving good-bye to the Titanic
and angrier still that i would sit
watching grainy pictures
shot from ambush
of small children
getting in and out of limousines

for this rude intrusion
i am truly sorry
but not for you

dear teacher
how can i be anything
but overjoyed
for someone
destined to spend eternity
aboard a great plumed ship
steaming out
across a bay of cobalt blue
you
at the rail
dreaming
forever leaning toward Orion

Looking for Georgia O'Keeffe

there are stories — horror stories!
and if the old woman were still alive
i would never have made the pilgrimage
to her Ghost Ranch residence

Bill Sozi
says she was anything but menacing
of course he is Native American
and a lunatic to boot
a painter of abstract buffalo
who thinks his head is on fire
and in the Southwest
no one pays attention to an artist
who isn't Gorman slick
or Di Grazia cute

no one
except perhaps Georgia O'Keeffe
at least
that's what i chose to believe
as i circled her remote adobe
a sneak thief window-peeking
stealing looks
through cracks in the blinds
a pair of red slippers —
the glimpse of an empty easel —
shadows on a stripped bed
and out back a ramada
black as a Penitente cross
against a sheet of high twilight sky

94

the enclosed garden overgrown
hollyhocks
broken down and gone to seed
brown patio walls hung
with the bleached bones
she had so lovingly rendered
and the view
i took that in too
filling my eyes
with the distant line of the Pedernal
floating above a sculpture
of salmon-colored hills

all the while
afraid that someone would come
and catch me making off
with this priceless ambience
Juan Hamilton
her protégé and beneficiary
arriving in a rage
to collar the robber — call the police

hurriedly
i picked a twig of sage
a remembrance
from the hem of the rutted driveway
and ran back to the car
back to the coast

where everything is close to Silicon Valley
and a hard copy
of an emotional experience like this
resembles the high country
about as much as a picture postcard
sent from Abiquiu, New Mexico

Pulitzer Prize Winner

of Louis Simpson i knew nothing
except that he had won the Pulitzer prize
for poetry

so when i saw that he also
was visiting the University of Michigan
i went to hear him read
to sit beforehand watching
while other interested students and faculty
trickled in chattering lightly nonchalant

amusing myself by trying to pick
our prize winner
out of the crowd up front
and while doing this realized
that everyone in the room
was the picture of a poet
young and flowing — old and fussy

finally
arriving down the aisle Simpson was there
looking like a certified public accountant
by the clock he took exactly
one hour of my time

afterward
crunching along
through a crisp Ann Arbor afternoon
i considered getting a haircut

Burnout—a Misnomer

burnout
you've seen the results
in the shop on the shelf
row after row of grey empty faces
with nothing happening in the glassy eyes
except
a little surface reflection

burnout
you know the symptoms
a history of dependable service
then suddenly for no reason things go dark
and you're a dead piece of furniture
waiting
to be removed from the living room

burnout
the psychological repairman said
and shrugged and shook his head
having checked everything
except the cord
which of course
was disconnected
in a word "unplugged"

and to think
i nearly went to the dump myself
because someone less than a poet
trying to describe a condition
came up with a misleading term
clearly
a case of burnout demands a second opinion
and this is mine
find an outlet
and if the cord doesn't reach
move the set

Happy Endings in the Badlands

two over-the-hill actors
still play tug of war
with your mask Kemo Sabe
not that they need the money
they don't
it's just that they won't
give up the tyranny of the dream—
silver bullets and white hats
are hard to let go of—
i know

there's lots of dust and excitement
surrounding the arrival and departure
of the Wells Fargo Stage—
lots of "yeah!" and "ya-hoo!"

however
out near the sixty-mile marker
at a complete standstill
the question arises
who drives the wagon
when ambition and necessity
no longer work for you?
when the grubstake days are over
and you've settled for something less
than being number one
who cracks the whip
and rides shotgun then?

enter the grinning bandido
enter what looks like the end
with pistol in hand
and instructions
to "kiss your *culo* good-bye"
and take it from me
it's not easy
to keep a positive attitude
with your life passing before your eyes
but
"what the hell"
i said to myself
if this is it i might as well
sit back and enjoy the show
which i did and while doing so
caught sight of a pilgrim
who looked a lot like me
doing what he wanted to do
going where he wanted to go
and making a living at it

or more precisely
being paid for the living he made
i mean
how lucky can you be?
and with that
the buckboard was back up to speed

who drives the wagon
when ambition and necessity
no longer work for you?
try gratitude
then cue the *William Tell* Overture
the Lone Ranger rides again!

Where the Poems Come From

to an idea of Robert Bly

it is dark
on the underside of morning
for me it is
and anxiety waits here
a cold-blooded reptile
coiled into a sluggish knot
a hunger that keeps the birds away
whispering
fear
fear
fear

i retreat
to exorcise with Barbara Walters
who became Jane Pauley
who becomes...
brewing coffee
and while doing this
watch the field from the window
sometimes a three-legged fox appears
not every day
but when she does
she kills and eats the lizard

and what i was feeling turns around
becoming what it always was

a tool to use
a wand to wave

till afternoon and evening vanish
and i can see the voice of a lark
an illusion — true
but one that sheds light on everything
and makes it look so easy

at least till
night descends
the capstone under which it all
begins again

A Farm Accident Years Ago

the horses shied and then wild-eyed
bolted from the field
racing back toward the barn
traces flying
the mower still attached
and running close behind
your father
shouting an alarm
as that ugly snapping arm
reached out
taking everything off at the ankle
weeds and corn and hollyhock
and then in slow motion
sweeping through the stems
of two small boys frozen in surprise

and sometime later
in a photograph we find
those grinning little peg-legged Petes
proud as punch
posing
though the color and shape
are exactly right
an artificial limb
is what it is
and can be put on and taken off
but the story that comes with it
walks
and walks and walks

106

Whales

off Palo Colorado

today i saw the whales
moving south along the coast
and had to stop the car and get out
and stand there just watching

one of them came in close to shore
and i thought to myself then
that the whole journey would be worth it
just to see the magic of this Atlantis — rising
blowing and steaming from the sea — an island
of life
today i saw the whales and i was healed

i can tell you now of the dancers — the three girls
and the dark wet highway — and the car
that came hurtling into their young lives
and how the rain fell for five days as we followed
slowly behind black limousines — three times
slowly with our lights on

but the sun returned this morning
and the rain has washed the air clean
and brought the Ventana mountains in so close
they cut my eyes
sometimes it hurts to see things clearly

for those girls the dance had just begun
but they went out dancing
trailing veils behind them and somehow
this simple act tells me that they too paused

somewhere along the way and saw
the whales moving south along the coast
on a day like today

i hope you will forgive me
for trying to put order and sense to it all
but if i don't can you tell me who in hell will?

Wailing Wall

i will be your wailing wall man-friend
lean on me and rail against the insanity
of life/death

we have lost one of our sons old soldier
hold on tight—hammer your fist—shout your curses
shit!

tell me how it was when last you saw him
your golden boy
wild hair flying—king of his mountain

beat on me—weep on me
old fighter
i will hold you up as you would me

later i will stack these words one upon the other
like stones lifted from my chest
and then fall sobbing against this wall of work

The Wasp Nest

it held my attention
like the ash on the end of Grandfather's cigar
taking shape slowly the way some poems do
the mind flying to and from it
unable to leave it alone

it hung in the eves
on the northeast corner of the house
a small grey planet
inhabited
industrious
a papier-mâché world parallel to mine
benign
until the child was stung

coexistence is no longer possible
hissed the canister
breathing violence
into the cells of this geodesic dome
and from deep within the abbey
a choir of small voices swelled
in a final
angry
ooooommmmmmmm
a sound
that clutched the evening air
like a hand sinking in a pool of silence

next morning i took a broom
and once again
the Hindenburg came down
like a cardboard head spilling its beaded brains
then sweeping up and burning the remains
i had intended to put the incident away

and would have
were it not for that tiny starship
coming in from a distant exploration
returning to the place where earth had been

and i could do nothing but sit at my window
my God's eye
watching the lone survivor cling to the moorings
having only himself now
as proof of something more
hanging on somehow
till the darkness took him

the wasp
who knew what it was to be human

From the Shore

an answer for Stevie Smith

i ain't waving babe, i'm drowning
going down in a cold lonely sea
i ain't waving babe, i'm drowning
so babe quit waving at me

i ain't laughing babe, i'm crying
i'm crying, oh why can't you see?
i ain't fooling babe, i ain't fooling
so babe quit fooling with me

this ain't singing babe, it's screaming
i'm screaming that i'm gonna drown
and you're smiling babe, and you're waving
just like you don't hear a sound

i ain't waving babe, i'm drowning
going down right here in front of you
and you're waving babe, you keep waving
hey babe, are you drowning too?

oh

Two Voices

for Sylvia Plath

poets are a skittish breed of cat
crouching in the doorway
we make our presence known
careful where we put our feet
we must be
for there is only one room in the house
and in it two voices
one that shouts
out cat out
the other calling
come kitty
pretty kitty

and there was this oversensitive Siamese
she could only hear the anti-voice
the dark one

but jesus she described it well
filling books with the pitch timber and tone
the awful sound
that hounded her childhood
ruined her youth
and finally chased her off
to curl up and die alone
in an envelope of natural gas

poor pitiful thing
shouted down by a half-truth

For Anne Sexton

Anne—i suffer the fate of a fan
i read your poems today
rode them like horses
magnificent beasts
and i was impressed with the way
you've harnessed your pain
with the way
you kept yourself sane
riding those
wild
twisting
dreams
down
to a standstill
down to a fanfare
admiring the way you could trot them around
under perfect control
no wonder they gave you
the prize
but the photograph on the dustcover
the cowpuncher face
the big floppy hat
i could have done without that
and the terrible hurt in your eyes

and now they tell me
you've gone down under the hooves
with Sylvia

Anne
was there ever a dream
couldn't be rode
or a dreamer
couldn't be throwed?

A California Mental Health Scene

trolling
the California mental health scene
with a two-day seminar: Depression Syndrome —
An Astrological Vegetarian Holistic Approach

the catch was for the most part
native to the Pacific coast
flounders — groupers
left in the wake of Prop. 13
what you might expect
except
for two migrating Easterners

a deepwater psychiatrist
who took copious notes in a perfect hand
his eyes had a bugged look
but under pressure his gaze never wavered
and
a female child psychologist
a spiny thing in a tailored tweed suit
who retreated into a hardcover book
whenever approached

even before orientation was over
they had found each other
and like sharks
formed a silent alliance

a disturbing presence
that had the rest of us running like grunion
darting around
intellectualizing
unable to risk and grow
knowing there was something alien
in the water
sizing us up
rolling its eyes
exchanging looks that ranged from pain
to pity
a couple of cold fish
in the house of Aquarius

next day however
the sea-world analogy
began to come apart
for the psychologist
it happened at coffee break
when mildly amused by something
she smiled
and in that brief softening
i could see that she was quite pretty

the psychiatrist?
he kept that pencil going
until just before noon
when he startled the room
with a Robert-Penn-Warren-type poem
about wanting to grow up
and be like his youngest son

after lunch they didn't return
somewhat relieved
and at the same time disappointed
the rest of us came together
for a warm California closing
ohmmmmmmm

what happened to them?
only they know
perhaps they went on
to spend the afternoon together
in San Francisco

two lonely people
three thousand miles from the ocean
living out
the kind of sophisticated story
you only find in the *New Yorker*

The Day of the Dogfish

July 1970
the night of the salmon bake
Tank Richards nearly OD'd
after which
the entire youth group
confessed to using dope
and was summarily expelled from the grounds
the older generation left behind
to wrestle with hypocrisy
"happy hour" in ruins
but then a successful conference
always needs
some real crisis to deal with
as Black Elk says
"where the path of difficulty
crosses the easy way
mark a holy place"

seventeen summers later
the incident
that would galvanize
the camp community appeared
almost laughable by comparison
it seems
some of the seventh-grade boys
had cornered and killed a dogfish
at the shallow end of the lagoon
and then chased the girls around
waving the carcass overhead

well—
you might have thought
civilization had collapsed then and there
the Dean instantly scheduling
an emergency meeting
to precede the evening's activities
(which
as fate would have it
was a memorial service
commemorating the anniversary
of the bombing of Hiroshima)

all campers will attend!
no one is excused!
and i as theme speaker
was chosen to try and put
the day of the dogfish to rest

to ask out loud
if what started out innocently enough—
a young fisherman
attempting to remove Jaws
(dogfish are small sharks)
from the swimming area—
turned into a killing frenzy?
one eyewitness said
he saw boys with sticks
stabbing and clubbing
till the water ran red

or was it
as others would insist
a rush to be humane
to put a mortally wounded creature
out of its misery and pain

an act of kindness?
an act of brutality?
like *Rashomon*
everyone saw
what they wanted to see

as for me
i remembered
the birthday boy
with his brand-new pellet gun
and the skunk
that began as a target —
a tin can —
but when hit transformed itself
into a living breathing thing
hurt and suffering
my weapon not powerful enough
for a clean kill
i shot and shot and shot
sickened and horrified
at the kaleidoscope of expression
in the dying animal's eyes
it was the death lesson
that haunts me still

122

as for the accusation
that using the fish
to tease the girls
showed somehow
that these young men
had little respect for life
prompted me to tell the story
about the time my own kids
were willing to die
trying to save Ol' Strut & Cluck
from the frying pan
my daughter Pocahontas
throwing herself
across the chopping block
then
even before the severed head
had hit the ground
triumphantly marching
the bloody squirming body around

my god!
it's the *Lord of the Flies*
i thought
until someone older and wiser
suggested that children
can make the transition
between something living
and something dead
more quickly than adults can

this event
these memories
dredging up the song i sang
decades ago
at antiwar demonstrations
a song that concluded

"you can multiply the lemming
till they rush into the sea
but what have suicidal rodents
got to do with you and me
we might have split the atom
but to worry is absurd
and yet
my son is in the garden
trying to kill a bird"

and recalling this
i also recalled
that once in a Unitarian church
a frenzy of angry women
demanded that i explain
my metaphor

and when they learned
that i had given my son
a BB gun for Christmas
they were upon me like barracuda
ripping and tearing
and just when it looked like
i was a goner for sure
a young stranger reached in
and hauled me out with this:

I was raised a Quaker
he said
forbidden even to have a friend
who owned a gun
and so
in my rebellious years
I declared my independence
by joining the Marines
and oh how I wish now
I could have learned about death
from a skunk a bird or a fish
you see the first thing I killed
was human

and that was the end of that
and this too
the camp community
filing out of the meeting house
and down to the lagoon
where we launched
our fleet of *toro*
floating paper lanterns
each one lit with a candle
to represent the soul
of a human being
who perished at Hiroshima

there on the shore we stood
singing hymns
clinging to one another
till time
extinguished every light
and in darkness we vanished
leaving the dogfish
to move instinctively
through their watery night

The Orangutans

on public television
there were pictures of a Canadian woman
a devoted naturalist
living in the rain forest of Sumatra

her husband
formerly her tracker
and a native of the region
was described
as having an uncanny ability
to locate wild orangutans
another woman
might have settled for a captain of industry

aside from the comic relief
however
this well-intentioned piece
was for the most part
standard
Beauty and the Beast

at least
for those of us who have been
to the Philadelphia zoo
and seen the caged gorilla
with such melancholy
etched into his giant face
we all wept openly
and this certainly looked
like more of the same

128

which it was
ending with our heroine
standing beneath the jungle canopy
looking up
trying to extend our apologies

the golden primates
last seen
climbing higher in the sad green trees
slowly pulling themselves up
hand over hand

A Kind of Hope

i guess you'd call him a revolutionary
but he laughed real laughter
and when he was quiet his eyes were sad
so i hung around and listened to him talk

he said
we have broken the ocean beyond repair
the crabs are leaving
we will soon follow

he said
we live in an insane asylum
where the sensitive go insane
that is to say go sane
and then must kill the pain
with pill and needle

he said
the next time the conquering heroes arrive
the future is gone in a nuclear flash

he said
and there is no time left for the corn
to grow

but the fact that he bothered to get out of bed
this morning and say it gives me
a kind of hope

Burning Truth

the mail comes
and i lose another friend today
to sweet Jesus

head bowed
i read the news written in your own hand
somehow antiseptic now
on the cleanest piece of paper
i have ever seen

praise be to God
praise God
over and over and over

you gave the answers
from beginning to end
with no space left
for walking mountain roads again
two men
talking in the twilight
playing with the questions

God knows
i need a crutch at times
to get this gimpy soul of mine around
but not a burning truth that we must
kill each other over

Even As We Speak

the future rises
like a swollen stream
the highway sinking in the flood
a pale arm up to its elbow
in a bad dream

like a mad dog
the rushing
water tears at our sleeves
we need another crossing
comparable to the one
that hung between two thieves

another skyway
whose bony framework
reaches in both directions
a poem
able to bear the weight of this fools' parade

and already
voices come from everywhere
gathering before us
in the electric air
even as we speak
the connection is being made

132

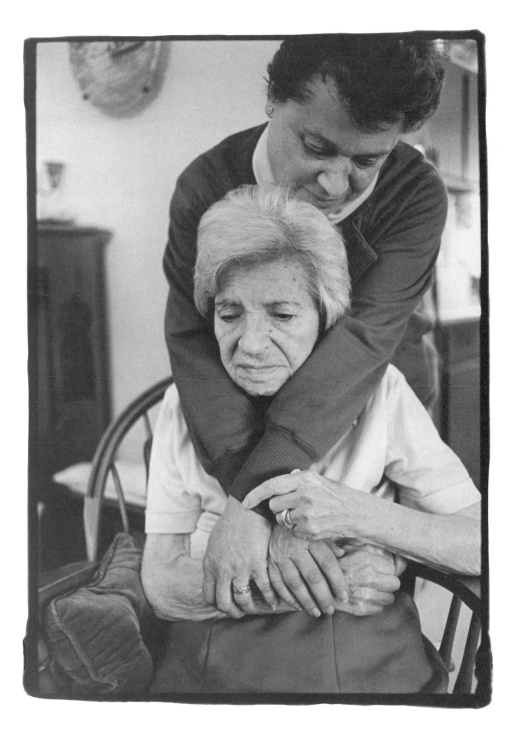

With a Friend Dying of Cancer

forty-nine and waiting
and what for
the bottom line

back in act one — scene one
it was obvious
we were waiting to see what would happen
but deeper into the drama
we recognize the antagonist
and realize there will be no "surprise" ending
which would seem to make it a farce

so i'll go with that a while
and tell about a comic
who built a career around a rickety ladder
and he was funny enough
to make us smile and forget

being silly is a noble occupation
so i fashioned some tomfoolery of my own
i really didn't know what i was doing
but i loved watching you go for it
coming by
gawking like a tourist
slowing down for a better view
then — WHAM!

i'd be there with a slapstick
clowning around in the death scene
doing pratfalls
waiting for the laughs
that's it!
that's what we're all waiting for
the end is always there
you can count on it
but the laughs
are few and far between

Let It Be a Dance

let it be a dance we do
may i have this dance with you
through the good times
and the bad times too
let it be a dance

let a dancing song be heard
play the music say the words
and fill the sky with sailing birds
and let it be a dance
learn to follow learn to lead
feel the rhythm fill the need
to reap the harvest plant the seed
and let it be a dance

everybody turn and spin
let your body learn to bend
and like a willow with the wind
let it be a dance
a child is born the old must die
a time for joy a time to cry
take it as it passes by
and let it be a dance

the morning star comes out at night
without the dark there can be no light
and if nothing's wrong then nothing's right
so let it be a dance

let the sun shine let it rain
share the laughter bare the pain
and round and round we go again
so let it be a dance

yes!
let it be a dance!
let life be a dance
because we dance to dance
not to go anywhere
and
let it be a dance!
let life be a dance
because within the dance
we move easily with the paradox
knowing
that for every step forward
there will be a step back
and anything else
would have us
marching away from the music

Afterword

After reading *The Thorn Birds*, I became aware I was like the woman who didn't realize she loved her husband until after he had died.

I dreamed about my sixteen-year-old boyfriend from high school who had rejected me but whom I'd carried around with me all these years. He came flying into my dream like the bridegroom in Chagall's painting, letting me know he was just a dream. If I met him today he'd be nearly sixty years old. I probably wouldn't recognize him or respect his politics. I woke up.

Listening to Ric read his poems, more so than any other person, has been a series of awakenings up for me. I learned life is a lot easier if you can go for the laughs. Whenever I had a problem he'd say, "Write about it." We talked and wrote our way out of breaking up our marriage at the twenty-year point. We now contract annually, a contract we composed. I have taken permission from his example to write, to have opinions and ideas, to critique, to grow. I find his work a source of inspiration.

I have been a witness to his perserverance, his dedication in logging his life-ideas into word poems. He is generous by nature, sharing with anyone who will listen. In the Boston airport, on our way to upper New York State to do readings for high school students, held up by the weather, Ric read poems to the other passengers, giving that captive audience some laughs, leaving them a bit more relaxed.

He is my best friend, a friend of the world. All he wants from you and me is for us to listen.

As his constant companion I haven't always been happy but I've never been bored, always as many laughs as tears.

I hope you let this book and tape give you permission to write, to do, to be all that's you.

BILLIE BARBARA MASTEN

About the Author

Ric Masten was born in Carmel, California, in 1929. He has toured extensively over the last twenty-five years, reading his poetry in more than 400 colleges in North America, Canada, and England. He is a well-known conference theme speaker and is a regular on many television and radio talk shows. He lives with his wife Billie Barbara just south of Carmel in the Big Sur mountains.

About the Photographer

Marianne Gontarz is a gerontological social worker and a professional photographer, combining her work in such photography projects as the Boston Women's Health Collective *Ourselves Growing Older*. Her photographs will illustrate *Aged to Perfection* (UCSF 1990) and *All About Aging* (Simon & Schuster 1990). She lives and works in Marin County, California.

About the Artist

Reed Farrington was born in 1938 in Parker, Arizona, and was raised and schooled on the Eastern seaboard, graduating from the United States Naval Academy in 1963, and the San Francisco Art Institute in 1970. His early influences were the California figure painters and the American Abstract Expressionists. He lives and paints in Big Sur, California.

Other available books by Ric Masten:

Looking for Georgia O'Keeffe	$6.50
Notice Me!	$6.00
They Are All Gone Now---And So Are You	$6.00
Even As We Speak	$5.50
The Deserted Rooster	$5.50
Stark Naked	$6.00
Voice of the Hive	$6.00
Dragonflies, Codfish, & Frogs	$6.00
His & Hers	$5.50

The above books may be ordered from Sunflower Ink, Palo Colorado Canyon, Carmel, CA 93923. California residents must include 6% sales tax. Please include $1.25 with each order for shipping.

Other Papier-Mache Press books:

When I Am an Old Woman I Shall Wear Purple	$10.00
If I Had a Hammer: Women's Work in Poetry and Fiction	$11.00
Fragments I Saved from the Fire: Stories by Mary Anne Ashley	$9.00
The Tie That Binds: Fathers & Daughters/Mothers and Sons	$10.00
Another Language: Poetry by Sue Saniel Elkind	$8.00
Flight of the Wild Goose: Poetry by Janet Carncross Chandler	$8.00
The Inland Sea: Poetry by Jenny Joseph	$5.00
Palm Coast: Prose-poem by Jim Martin	$8.00
Atalanta: An Anthology of Creative Work Celebrating Women's Athletic Achievements	$4.00
More Golden Apples: A Further Celebration of Women and Sport	$5.95

Support independent publishers and booksellers by ordering through your local independent bookstore or direct from Papier-Mache Press, 795 Via Manzana, Watsonville, CA 95076, (408) 726-2933.